**Teaching Guide**

# A Kid's Mensch Handbook

## Step by Step to a Lifetime of Jewish Values

**Tina Finck**

Springfield, New Jersey
www.behrmanhouse.com

Editor: Scott E. Blumenthal

Design: Itzhack Shelomi

ISBN: 0-874-41701-5

www.behrmanhouse.com

Manufactured in the United States of America

# Contents

# Introduction

## Introduction to the Textbook

*A Kid's Mensch Handbook* invites your students to explore timeless Jewish values in an accessible, modern, and exciting way. Through real-life examples, interactive activities, and a wealth of Jewish wisdom, *A Kid's Mensch Handbook* helps your students to make ethical choices, take positive actions, and treat all people (including themselves) with integrity and respect.

With *A Kid's Mensch Handbook*, you can provide your students with the knowledge and understanding to help foster Jewish values in their everyday lives. At the same time, the textbook will enrich your students' Jewish identities and connection to the Jewish community.

## Structure of the Textbook

*A Kid's Mensch Handbook* is divided into three sections:

I. "The Mensch Basics" introduces the definition of a mensch: a good person, a person of integrity and respect. Each of us affects the world in profound ways; a mensch is someone who makes choices and takes action that affects the world in *positive* ways. Jewish sources, experience, and wisdom serve as guides to becoming *menschen*.

II. "Be a Mensch to Yourself" examines ways that introspection and self-examination can lead to self-respect, and how self-respect can lead to respect for others. This section includes discussions of *b'tzelem Elohim*—the concept of being "created in God's image"—and *sh'mirat habriyut*—the mitzvah of caring for one's health.

III. "Be a Mensch to Others" explores ways to treat others with respect, generosity, and compassion. This section includes discussions of *talmud Torah*, "Jewish learning"; *sh'lom bayit*, "peace in the home"; *dibbuk haverim*, "attachment to friends"; and *k'vod habriyot*, "respect for all people."

For a detailed breakdown of each chapter's lesson and core concept, see the Scope and Sequence on page 8 of this Teaching Guide.

*A Kid's Mensch Handbook* also contains the following recurring features:

- **Mensch-Wise** Thought-provoking questions exercise skills in critical thinking.

- **Mensch Spotlight** Profiles of role models from Jewish history strengthen the link between the chapter and students' daily lives.

- **Top 5** Short interactive activities based on the main topic of each chapter help students apply Jewish values to their own lives.

- **Under the Mensch-ifying Glass** Definitions of key Hebrew terms clarify the meaning of core Jewish values.

- **A Note of Middot** Explorations of *middot*—virtues—related to the chapter's main Jewish value help students to become *menschen* with timeless, practical advice.

> **Note:** Izzy the Mensch-in-Training (the red-head cartoon character) appears throughout *A Kid's Mensch Handbook*, offering his wide-eyed commentary. Izzy's role is to amuse the students in the interest of enhancing their overall pleasure in the book and in Jewish learning. Allow students to giggle with him, give him funny voices, and enjoy watching him "grow up" as the book progresses.

## Structure of the Teaching Guide

The Teaching Guide closely follows the structure of *A Kid's Mensch Handbook*. There are nine chapters in the Teaching Guide, corresponding to each chapter of the textbook. Each chapter in the Teaching Guide contains sets of questions and answers that follow the main subject headings in the textbook.

> **Note:** *A Kid's Mensch Handbook* provides opportunities for your students to learn by sharing their opinions and personal experiences with one another. This Teaching Guide contains open-ended questions to help you enhance this experience and keep the discussion focused and productive.

Each chapter of this Teaching Guide contains the following features:

- **Overview** A brief statement summarizing the chapter's central governing idea.
- **Learning Objectives** Specific goals for

each chapter that correspond to the concepts and ideas that students should understand when they complete the chapter.

- **Vocabulary** Key terms and definitions from each chapter to use as oral review or with flash cards.
- **Set Induction** An initial thought or activity, based on core concepts from the chapter, to begin teaching the chapter materials.

In addition, each chapter in this Teaching Guide contains many of the following features:

- **Expand the Conversation** Questions and exercises to encourage students to further explore ideas and information presented in the textbook. Look for the icon.
- **Bring It to Life** Supplemental activities to reinforce and extend textbook learning. Look for the icon.
- **Photo Op** Ideas and techniques for using the textbook's photographs to stimulate conversation and reflection on the chapter's content. Look for the icon.
- **As a Family** Home-based activities to engage the whole family and reinforce classroom learning. Look for the icon.

# Before You Begin...

Here are some thoughts to keep in mind as you begin using *A Kid's Mensch Handbook*:

- *Foster a sense of security and fellowship.* Make it clear that your classroom is a safe space where students will be heard with respect and be guided, not judged. When a student prefers not to share, please respect his or her privacy.

- *Be aware.* Your students will come to class from a variety of backgrounds and experiences. Some students will have the maturity to manage emotions well; others will not. Teach all of your students to see Jewish values as a supportive guide to making life's tough decisions.

- *Include your students' parents along the way.* Many of the discussions and exercises in *A Kid's Mensch Handbook* lend themselves to parent participation and family learning. The "As a Family" features in this Teaching Guide provide ideal opportunities to "close the circuit" between class and home.

**Note:** Writing may be difficult for some students. You might invite individual students to do the written exercises without concern for grammar or spelling. If it seems helpful, you can also allow them to represent their ideas in pencil drawings or cartoons.

# Working with Students with Special Needs

Children vary in their learning styles. Some students learn best with a hands-on approach, while others do best with a visual or an auditory approach. In general, teachers who present material in many different ways will be able to reach many more children.

Teachers of children with special needs have extra challenges. These children may have a broad range of cognitive, physical, and behavioral disabilities that impact learning. It is always helpful to find out from parents what accommodations are made for their child in secular school. The suggestions included below are primarily for those children with learning, perceptual, or attention problems.

For students with attention and auditory processing problems, teach in small increments and present one instruction at a time. Ask the children to repeat the instruction to be sure they have processed it.

For children with attention problems, limit teaching segments to 10 to 15 minutes and allow for movement between activities.

For children with decoding problems, make flash cards with a few key words. Children can take them home and practice reading them with their parents. Keep a shoe box of flash cards for children who need them.

Provide opportunities for choral reading rather than asking children to read aloud individually.

For children with attention and visual figure-ground problems, mask parts of the page so they can see only the section that is being worked on.

For children with fine motor and handwriting problems, limit the amount of writing, drawing, and cutting that is required. The teacher or assistant may do difficult parts of a project and allow the student to finish the task.

# Scope and Sequence

Each chapter of *A Kid's Mensch Handbook* examines a core concept that serves as the chapter's main theme:

| Chapter | Pages | Core Concept |
|---|---|---|
| 1 | 8–13 | Each of us affects the world in profound ways. A mensch is someone who takes action that is generous and kind, action that affects the world in *positive* ways. |
| 2 | 14–23 | It is important to make good, ethical choices. Jewish sources, experience, and wisdom can help us to determine and make good choices. |
| 3 | 24–35 | Once we've made good choices, we must take action. An important guide to taking "mensch action" is The Golden Rule: *v'ahavta l'reacha kamocha*—love your neighbor as yourself. |
| 4 | 38–49 | We respect ourselves because we are created *b'tzelem Elohim*—in God's image. When we understand how it feels to respect *ourselves*, we better understand how *others* feel when we respect them. |
| 5 | 50–61 | We exercise self-respect through *sh'mirat habriyut*—guarding one's health. By caring for our bodies and our minds, we better prepare ourselves to be *menschen* to others. |
| 6 | 64–75 | A good way to learn how to treat others respectfully is through *talmud Torah*—Jewish learning. *Talmud Torah* may be the most important mitzvah of all, because learning leads to action. |
| 7 | 76–87 | We practice treating others respectfully with the value of *sh'lom bayit*—peace in the home. Through *sh'lom bayit*, we learn the qualities of forgiveness, responsibility, and patience. |
| 8 | 88–99 | We learn to treat friends and classmates respectfully with the value of *dibbuk ḥaverim*—attachment to friends. Through *dibbuk ḥaverim*, we help one another to be our best selves and reach our greatest potential. |
| 9 | 100–111 | We can show respect for all people through the values of *k'vod habriyot*—respect for all people; *derech eretz*—good manners; *klal Yisrael*—support for the world Jewish community; and *tzedakah*—righteousness. |
| Special Sections | 112–118 | We can review what we've learned with "Mensch Magic," "Mensch Diploma," and the "Handy-Dandy Mensch Index." |

# Part One

# The Mensch Basics

# Welcome to A Kid's Mensch Handbook

**Student text: pages 8–13**

## Overview

Chapter 1 introduces the book's theme: Like a stone dropped into a still lake, our actions affect the world around us. A mensch is someone who takes action and affects the world in positive ways. Chapter 1 also outlines the book's content and structure.

## Learning Objectives

Students will be able to:

- Describe how our actions "ripple out" and affect others.
- Define "mensch" and articulate qualities that characterize a mensch.
- Explain the book's contents and basic structure.

## Vocabulary

**mensch** "person"; someone of integrity and respect

## Set Induction

Have your students brainstorm a list of qualities that describe a good person. Write the list on the board. Start the exercise by writing *kindness, honesty,* and *respect.*

Ask each student to choose the three qualities he or she considers most important. Invite volunteers to share their choices, including reasons why they consider their qualities important.

## Making Waves (pages 9–10)

Have volunteers read the two paragraphs on page 9. Ask: What are some examples of actions that affect others? You may wish to have students share examples of the ways they have affected others positively and explain what they learned from the experience.

## Expand the Conversation

Have a student read the "Quick Quote" on page 9 aloud. Ask: What is the difference between wisdom and kindness? (*Wisdom has to with* knowledge *and* judgment; *kindness has to do with* action.)

## Photo Op

Point to the photo of the ripple on page 9. Have a student read the legend around the ripple ("The Stone," "Your Family," etc.). Explain that we'll see this image recur throughout *A Kid's Mensch Handbook* as a reminder that like a stone on a lake, our actions affect the world around us.

## That's Fine and Dandy (page 10)

Ask a volunteer to read the first paragraph of "That's Fine and Dandy" aloud. Students can alternate reading the bulleted items and then add definitions of their own.

## Too Many to Menschen (page 11)

As your students complete this exercise, direct them to include kind and generous *actions* taken by their *menschen*.

Invite the class to share their personal *menschen* with the class.

## Baby Mensch (page 12)

Have a volunteer read "Baby Mensch" aloud. Following is the full talmudic legend to share with the class:

> While a child is still in its mother's womb, it learns the entire Torah by the light of a special lamp that allows the baby to see everything on earth. When the baby is born, an angel appears and requires the baby to take an oath that he or she will live a life of righteousness. The angel then tweaks the baby's nose, causing it to forget everything it has learned. It then spends its life not learning new information, but "remembering" what it once knew.

Explain that this legend also provides a creative explanation for the furrow beneath our nostrils!

## As a Family

Copy and distribute "Family Worksheet 1" found on the following page. Ask students to complete the chart with their families.

During the next class session, have students present their charts to the class. Or, invite your students' parents to class to share the charts as a family. It's a great way to bring your students' families together.

**Family Worksheet 1**

# Too Many to Menschen: Family Version

Dear Parent:

This year, we will be studying Jewish values with our new textbook, *A Kid's Mensch Handbook*. Periodically we will send home a Family Worksheet based on lessons from the book for your family to complete together.

This week we learned that a *mensch* is a good person—a person of kindness, integrity, and respect. As a family, think of three people you consider *menschen* (plural of mensch): a family friend or neighbor, a teacher or community leader, and someone who is famous. Write their names on the lines below, then write down the reasons why each one is a mensch.

| Names: | | |
|---|---|---|
| Friend or Neighbor | Teacher or Community Leader | Someone Who Is Famous |

| Reasons each one is a mensch: | | |
|---|---|---|
| | | |

# Making Mensch Choices

**Student text: pages 14–23**

## Overview

Chapter 2 explores the importance of making good, ethical choices. We learn that all of us should participate in the ongoing quest for good choices.

## Learning Objectives

Students will be able to:

- Describe how their choices affect themselves and others.
- Explain how the Tanach, Talmud, and *midrashim* provide valuable guidance today, just as they did for our ancestors.
- Explain how good choices lead to positive action.

## Vocabulary

**hachnasat orḥim** "bringing in guests"; the mitzvah to welcome visitors and strangers

**midrash** "interpretation"; discussions and explanations of Jewish law and culture

**Talmud** "learning"; anthology of rabbinic law and lore

**Tanach** acronym (T.N.K.) for the three parts of the Hebrew Bible: the Torah (five books of Moses), Nevi'im (Prophets), and K'tuvim (Writings)

## Set Induction

Have each of your students recall the hardest choice he or she ever had to make. (Explain that these should be ethical dilemmas, not preferences, like the choice between vanilla and chocolate.) Ask:

- What made the choice so difficult?
- Were you pleased with the outcome?
- If presented with the same situation now, would you make the same choice?

Invite students to share their tough choices with the class. Then have students open their books to page 15. Explain that the class will now work through a tough choice *together*.

## The New-Kid Dilemma, Part 1
### (page 15)

Have a volunteer read "The New-Kid Dilemma, Part 1" aloud. Each student should answer the question at the bottom of the page: What would *you* choose to do? Encourage students to think in terms of good choices, as opposed to what others might think.

## The New-Kid Choice Chart
### (page 16)

After someone reads the title and directions aloud, students can work individually to complete the exercise. (Obviously, choice A leads to the more positive results.) Point out that making good choices does not always lead to a positive result, but making bad choices almost never does.

If time allows, invite students to share their "best friend" stories with the class.

## Bring It to Life

For fun, have students make a skit of "The New-Kid Choice Chart." Assign four students to play the parts of Alex and the three kids at the table. Have them perform the three scenarios:

1. Alex says no.

2. Alex says yes and moves to your table.

3. Alex continues to eat alone.

To include more students, assign four different students for each scenario.

## The Choice Is Yours (page 17)

Have volunteers read page 17 aloud. Ask your students to respond to the rhetorical questions in the middle of the page (Does dropping coins in the tzedakah box make a difference? Etc.). Guide students to compare answers with one another; this will illustrate the challenge of making good choices, and the fact that there is not always a perfect answer.

## Expand the Conversation

After your students have read the final paragraph, ask: What do you have in common with people who lived hundreds of years ago, and with those who will live hundreds of years from now? (*Answers may include: We have the same relationships: parents, siblings, friends, and neighbors; we all suffer sickness; we all grieve and cry when someone dies.*)

## Expand the Conversation

Have a student read the "Quick Quote" on page 17 aloud. Ask: In what way are our "days like scrolls"? (*We write our own "stories" with the choices we make.*)

## Three Cheers, Three Jeers
### (page 18)

Before your students complete this exercise, explain that they should think of their "not-so-good choices" not as mistakes, but as opportunities to learn how to make good choices in the future.

## Good Choice! (pages 19–20)

As your students read this section, interject the following questions:

- After paragraph 2 on page 19, ask: What are some other choices that we just *stumble* on? (*Answers may include: putting on a jacket when it's cold outside; wearing a seat belt; working hard in school.*)

- After paragraph 3 on page 19, ask: Should a person who injures another pay a fine, or receive the same injury? What do you think? Explain your answer. Again, encourage a comparison of ideas.

- After the paragraphs at the top of page 20, ask: Even if we don't find answers for some tough choices, why is it important to continue trying? Encourage students to respect an individual, even when disagreeing with his or her opinion.

If students express interest, let them discuss one or more of the bulleted questions on page 20. Again, there are no absolute answers; the process of making a good choice based on compassion and respect is what counts.

## Mensch-Wise (page 20)

Before your students begin this exercise, ask: How can emotions such as anger and jealousy affect our ability to make good choices? Have students consider this as they complete the exercise.

## Torah, Talmud, and Beyond
(page 21)

Have volunteers read page 21 aloud. Tell the class that they are about to create their own *midrashim.*

Remind students of the story of the Golden Calf from Exodus. (As the Israelites waited impatiently for Moses to descend from Mount Sinai, they forged a golden idol.) Ask: Why did the children of Israel choose to do such a thing? *(Answers may include: They became impatient; they didn't believe God would help them; they wanted to put their faith in something they could see and touch.)* Say: You've just helped to create a *midrash*!

## The New-Kid Dilemma, Part 2
(page 22)

Ask: In what ways can *you* welcome guests and strangers at your school? *(Answers may include: sharing a snack; including them in activities at recess; introducing them to classmates.)*

## Wisdom from the Old Country
(page 23)

After eight volunteers each read one of the Yiddish proverbs inside the bubbles on page 23, ask students to provide an example of how each proverb teaches them to make good choices. For example, "Too much of anything is unhealthy" reminds us not to overindulge— in TV, or food, or sleep.

*Note:* Before students complete the exercise at the bottom of page 25, you might explain that salt stings when it touches an open scratch or cut.

## As a Family

With their families, students can create their own "Good Choice Chart." Instruct your students:

- Have each member of your household list three good choices he or she has made in the past year. (Explain that "good" does not necessarily mean "successful.") It can be a simple act, such as helping around the house, or a daily habit, like choosing to recycle.

- As a family, discuss your lists. Why do you consider them good choices? Were you pleased with the outcome?

During the next class session, ask your students to share one or two good choices their families made.

# Taking Mensch Actions

Student text: pages 24–35

## Overview

In Chapter 3, we learn that once we've made good choices, we must perform positive actions, or *mitzvot*. One of the most important *mitzvot* is *v'ahavta l'reacha kamocha*, "love your neighbor as yourself."

## Learning Objectives

Students will be able to:

- Discuss why it is important to follow good choices with positive action.
- Define *mitzvot*, understand why they are important, and provide several examples.
- Explain the meaning of The Golden Rule and how it leads to all other *mitzvot*.

## Vocabulary

**bikkur holim** the mitzvah to visit the sick

**kavod** "respect"

**leiv tov** "a good heart"; generosity

**l'shon hara** "the evil tounge"; the value of avoiding gossip

**middah** value or virtue (plural: *middot*)

**mitzvah** "commandment"; an ethical or ritual obligation; any act of kindness or generosity (plural: *mitzvot*)

**rodef shalom** the mitzvah to "pursue peace"

**tzedakah** "righteousness"; the mitzvah to give to those in need

**v'ahavta l'reacha kamocha** "love your neighbor as yourself"; The Golden Rule

## Set Induction

Call pairs of volunteers to the front of the classroom to act out the following two scenes:

1. Have Student A drop a pencil on the floor. Have Student B *choose* to pick up the pencil for Student A, but take no action. (Tell Student B to wish very, very hard.)

2. Have Student A drop a pencil to the floor. Tell Student B to choose to pick up the pencil, then actually pick it up and give it to Student A.

Ask the class:

- What was the difference between the two scenes?

- Was Student B in the first scene a mensch? (*We don't know; he or she didn't do anything.*)

- What does this exercise teach us about being a mensch? (*In order to be a mensch, we must take action.*)

## Starting Small (pages 25–26)

You may wish to turn this dialogue into a short play. Assign students the parts of the narrator, Rachel, her big brother, and their grandmother. (To make it easier, point out that Rachel speaks in the first paragraph, then in every other paragraph after that. The big brother speaks in the second paragraph, then the grandmother in every other paragraph after that.)

Ask the class:

- What is the difference between Rachel and her grandmother's approaches to helping the hungry? (*Rachel thinks in big, ambitious terms, but does nothing. Rachel's grandmother plans to take small steps.*)

- Whose approach do you think is better? Why? Encourage your students to think in terms of which approach leads to *action*.

- Of the three specific plans that Rachel and her grandmother make, which will help people to help themselves? (*The third plan—donating seeds, so that the people can feed themselves.*)

 ## Expand the Conversation

Have a student read the "Quick Quote" at the bottom of page 26 aloud. Ask: How is wisdom without action like a tree without fruit? (*We cannot benefit from it unless it is something we see, feel, experience, etc.*)

Have your students think of other analogies by finishing the sentence: Wisdom without action is like _____. Allow your students to have fun with this exercise, as long as it reinforces the point that action is vital.

## The Mitzvah Marvel (page 27)

Explain that *mitzvah* literally means *commandment*. In its broadest sense, we may consider any act of kindness or generosity a mitzvah.

As your students complete the exercise, remind them that there are many ways to perform *mitzvot* (plural of mitzvah).

Invite students to share their answers with the class.

## Mitzvah Your Way to Mensch-hood (page 28)

If time permits, allow students to share personal examples of *mitzvot* they've performed—today, this week, and in the past.

## Photo Op

Point to the photo of the boy at summer camp on page 28. Have a volunteer read the caption aloud. Ask: What are some other opportunities to perform *mitzvot* at summer camp? (*Answers may include: cleaning the bunk, being kind to our campmates, sticking up for kids who are being picked on.*)

Explain that wherever we may be, there are opportunities to perform *mitzvot*.

## A Vote for Mitzvot (page 29)

Ask: How does your "mensch radar" help you recognize an opportunity for a mitzvah? Encourage your students to consider the importance of paying attention to others and their needs.

## A Mitzvah a Day (page 29)

After students have completed their exercises, invite volunteers to read their lists aloud. Write the *mitzvot* on the board. Then have students think of as many "everyday *mitzvot*" as they can. Each student should choose (either aloud or privately) one new mitzvah from the list that he or she will perform every day, starting now. Leave the list on the board.

## Expand the Conversation

Read this passage from the Torah to your students:

> The commandments are not difficult or far away...they are close to you, in your mouth, and in your heart.
>
> (DEUTERONOMY 30:11–14)

Ask: What do you think this quote means? (*Answers may include:* Mitzvot *don't have to be hard; there are always* mitzvot *to perform; everyone has the power to perform* mitzvot.)

## Mensch Spotlight (page 31)

For fun, have students read this "Mensch Spotlight" by having them pretend to be newscasters, reporting a breaking story. Assign an anchor to read *Name* and *Scene*, one reporter to read *Action*, and another reporter to read *What made Naḥshon a mensch* and *It's a fact.*

Ask students to describe examples from their own experience of times when they overcame doubts or difficulties to take action, even when no one else did.

## On One Foot (pages 32–33)

After reading the passage, refer to the list of "everyday *mitzvot*" on the board. Point to each one and ask: Does this help you to love your neighbor as yourself? The answer to most—or all—should be yes.

Explain that starting here, every chapter will contain a Jewish value in Hebrew, including an "Under the Mensch-ifying Glass" discussion of the Hebrew words themselves.

Ask the class to read the Hebrew inside the magnifying glass aloud. Ask: Where in the prayer service do we find the first word? What does the word mean? (*In the V'ahavta, after the Sh'ma, when we remind ourselves that "you will love" Adonai your God...*)

## One More Time! (page 34)

Before your students complete this exercise, ask them to think of arguments they've had in their lives. Ask them to think about:

- Why did the argument start?
- Why did the argument continue?
- Who ended the argument? How? Why?

## A Note of Middot: Generosity (page 35)

Have a volunteer read the paragraph at the top of page 35. To demonstrate how *middot* work, have volunteers say "I'm sorry" in two ways: (1) as a genuine apology, and (2) a sarcastic "Sor-*ree.*" Ask: What is the difference between the two? Which kind helps make someone a mensch?

Have volunteers read the rest of the page. Ask: Why is *leiv tov* important in the classroom? At home? In the community? Ask your students to think of instances—when we are upset, or sick, or hungry—when we rely on one another's generosity.

 ## As a Family

Direct your students to perform a special mitzvah at home in the coming week—one they don't normally perform. Suggest that they put away groceries, fold the laundry, collect and take out the trash, or any other action that will illustrate the mitzvah of *v'ahavta l'reacha kamocha*—love your neighbor (in this case, your family) as yourself.

During the next class session, ask: What mitzvah did you perform? How did your parents react? What did you learn from this mitzvah?

# Part Two

# Be a Mensch to Yourself

## Chapter 4

# Seeing Yourself as a Mensch

**Student text: pages 38–49**

## Overview

In Chapter 4, we learn that we are created *b'tzelem Elohim*—in the image of God—and therefore should treat ourselves with respect. Once we respect *ourselves*, we better understand how to respect *others*.

## Learning Objectives

Students will be able to:

- Discuss why it is important to examine ourselves and to challenge ourselves to take positive actions.

- Understand what it means to be created *b'tzelem Elohim*—in the image of God.

- Provide examples of ways to practice self-respect, including personal reflection, honesty with oneself, and prayer.

## Vocabulary

***b'tzelem Elohim*** "in the image of God"

***nefesh*** the soul; the spiritual quality that sets human beings apart from other creatures

***t'filah*** "prayer"

## Set Induction

Ask your students to make a list of words or phrases that describe people who respect themselves. Write the list on the board. Begin the list with the word *mensch*. Leave the list on the board for the remainder of the lesson.

## The Mensch-Cam (page 39)

After students read the entire page, ask:

- What does it mean to be "the hero—and the author—of your life story"? (*We can choose our own actions, which in turn affect those around us.*)

- Why is it important to examine our actions? (*To make sure that we make good choices and take positive actions—mensch actions.*)

### Expand the Conversation

Have a volunteer read the "Quick Quote" at the bottom of page 39 aloud. Ask: Why must we "become a blessing to ourselves" in order to "be a blessing to others"? Explain that if we respect ourselves, we are more likely to treat others with respect.

## Mensch Movie Review (page 40)

Make sure your students understand that each person's "mensch movie" includes actions they've taken during the past week. Remind your students: The hero of each mensch movie is you!

## An Eye That Sees (page 41)

Tell your students that the quote from *Pirkei Avot* is part of a larger passage, which asks: "What is the straight path a person should choose?" *Pirkei Avot* teaches us that God pays attention to our actions, but we are still responsible for our choices.

### Bring It to Life

Explain that there are many ways to see oneself. To illustrate this point, have your students cover their eyes. Ask: What do you see? *(Answers will vary.)* Then ask: How do you see yourself? Allow students to keep their answers private.

## I Know What You Mean (page 41)

Spend a few minutes discussing the sentence, "When we understand how it feels to respect *ourselves*, we better understand how others feel when we respect *them*." Explain that even though we may not have shared the same experiences as others, we all know how it feels to be happy, sad, and lonely. As a result, we know how important it is to be sensitive to other people's feelings.

## In God's Image (page 42)

Have a student read the Hebrew inside the "Mensch-ifying Glass" aloud. Read the passage from the Torah where the phrase first appears:

> And God created the human in God's image…male and female God created them. And God blessed them and said to them, "Be fruitful and multiply and fill the earth…." (GENESIS 1:27–28)

## The Breath of Life (page 43)

After each bulleted item, ask your students to share examples of times when *they* were "like God." *(Examples may include: reciting blessings over Shabbat candles; writing a story or painting a picture; standing up for a younger sibling.)*

## Two Pockets (page 44)

Ask your students:

- What would life be like if we only believed "For me the world was created"? *(We would become self-centered or unaware of other people's feelings.)*
- What would life be like if we only believed "I am but dust and ashes"? *(We would become overly negative and lose self-respect.)*

Remind students that it is important to find a balance between the two.

## B'tzelem Elohim Top 5
### (pages 45–48)

Explain that each of the next five chapters will include a "Top 5" list, with ideas, suggestions, and tips for bringing that chapter's Jewish value to life.

> **Note:** In order to help students enjoy the exercises and create more positive associations with the material, allow for a more relaxed, informal atmosphere—within reason, of course—while reviewing these "Top 5" exercises. Perhaps have the class arrange their chairs in a circle, or even sit outside.

**A Kid's Mensch Handbook · Teaching Guide**

## 1. Take Stock

Explain that there are no right or wrong answers to this *b'tzelem Elohim* quiz. The object is to be honest with yourself, in order to evaluate our actions.

## 2. Be Kind

Challenge your students to make a personal pledge: I will go out of my way to be an extra-kind person this week.

## 3. Be Yourself

Remind your students that according to Jewish belief, each person was born for a special purpose. Rather than trying to be someone else, we should each be the best person we can be!

## 4. Recharge Your Batteries

If your students ask for more guidance, encourage them to draw or write about a favorite place, book, or memory.

## 5. Speak with God

Encourage students to think of prayer services in a different way—as an opportunity to reflect on their day and their week, and to think of ways they can be even more of a mensch.

## A Note of Middot: Contentment
**(page 49)**

Tell your students that in Hebrew, this *middah* is *sameaḥ b'ḥelko*—"happy with one's lot." (They may recognize the word *simḥah*, "happy," as in "a happy occasion.")

Ask: In what ways are you happy with your lot? Tell students to think about all the reasons

they have to be grateful. Focus on blessings that are not material, such as family, friends, and health.

## As a Family

Copy and distribute the "Family Worksheet" found on the following page. Instruct students to complete the exercise with their families. During the next class session, have students share their charts with the class.

**Family Worksheet 2**

# Happy with One's Lot

Dear Parent:

In *A Kid's Mensch Handbook* we learned that according to Jewish tradition we are created *b'tzelem Elohim*—in the image of God—and therefore should treat ourselves with respect. Once we respect *ourselves*, we better understand how to respect *others*.

## Part I

As a family, read this Jewish legend aloud:

> The students of Reb Zusya came to their teacher, who lay dying. They were surprised to see him trembling with fear.
>
> "Why are you afraid of death?" they asked. "In your life, have you not been as righteous as Moses himself?"
>
> "When I stand before the throne of judgment," Zusya answered, "I will not be asked, 'Reb Zusya, why were you not like Moses?' I will be asked, 'Reb Zusya, why were you not like Zusya?'"

It's hard to respect yourself if you're trying to be someone else. "Who is rich?" the sages asked. "The one who is happy with one's lot."

## Part II

As a family, list reasons why each of *you* is happy with who you are.

| Name of Family Member | Reasons I am happy with who I am |
| --- | --- |
|  |  |
|  |  |
|  |  |
|  |  |

# Chapter 5

# Treating Yourself as a Mensch

**Student text: pages 50–61**

## Overview

In Chapter 5, we learn that an important way to exercise self-respect is through *sh'mirat habriyut*—guarding one's health. By caring for our bodies and our minds, we better prepare ourselves to be *menschen* to others.

## Learning Objectives

Students will be able to:

- Define and discuss the value of *sh'mirat habriyut*—guarding one's health.

- Explain how our choices affect our bodies and minds.

- Make healthful choices, based on Jewish wisdom and experience.

## Vocabulary

***sh'mirat habriyut*** "guarding one's health"

## Set Induction

Divide the class into groups of 3 or 4. Write the following quote from Maimonides on the board: "The body is the instrument of the soul." Ask: What do you think this quote means? In what ways is the body the "instrument of the soul"? Give the groups 5 minutes

to discuss their answers.

Then have each group present its conclusion to the class. Explain that this chapter will discuss the importance of treating our bodies—and our minds—with respect.

## Squeaky Brakes (page 51)

Ask: Had you been the child in the story, what would you have done differently? *(Answers may include: I would not have left the bicycle out in the rain; I would not have left the bicycle in the driveway.)*

Then ask: How is taking care of a bicycle like taking care of your body? *(Both require care, maintenance, and attention.)*

## Dr. Goodmensch (page 52)

As your students complete this exercise, explain that for centuries cleanliness and attention to one's diet have been important Jewish values.

For each Rx pad, encourage students to think of specific ways to help each patient—perhaps by joining a sports team, paying attention in class, or eating an apple a day.

## Hillel's Mitzvah (page 53)

Have two volunteers act out the exchange between Hillel and his student. (The student reads the first paragraph, Hillel the second, then they alternate.)

Ask: Why is it more important to care for our bodies than for a statue? *(Answers may include:*

*A statue does not require care to live; we are created in God's image, while a statue is not; caring for ourselves is a mitzvah.)*

## Photo Op

Have a student read the photo caption at the bottom of page 53. Ask: What's *your* favorite healthful food? Take a poll to find the class's favorite fruit and favorite vegetable.

## Be a Body Mensch (page 54)

After reading this section, ask a student to read the Hebrew phrase that appears under the "Mensch-ifying Glass."

Tell your students that *sh'mirat* comes from the Hebrew word for "guard." They may be interested to know that a babysitter is called a *shomer-taf*, a "guardian of children."

## Bring It to Life

Begin a new class tradition: When someone sneezes, have their classmates say, "*Labriyut!*"

## All in the Mind (page 55)

Illustrate the close relationship between our bodies and minds with the following scenarios:

1. It's one hour before bedtime. You've got a big test tomorrow, and your spelling is still rusty. But you're having so much fun playing your newest video game. What do you do?

2. You've just come home from religious school and you're *really hungry*. Dinner will be ready in half an hour, but the cookie jar is full—and no one's looking.

Ask students to describe the results of each possible action, and how the actions will affect their bodies.

## Expand the Conversation

Choose a volunteer to read aloud the "Quick Quote" at the bottom of page 55. Read more of the passage from Proverbs: "A clever mind seeks knowledge, the mouth of a foolish person pursues foolishness." Ask: What do you think this quote means? *(Answers may include: It is important to learn; we should always ask questions; we should not assume that we know everything.)*

## Body-ography (page 56)

Have students complete this exercise individually. If time allows, ask volunteers to read their answers aloud. Challenge your students to fulfill their "Looking Ahead" resolutions in the coming week.

## Mensch Spotlight (page 57)

Have your students describe how *sh'mirat habriyut* helped Yael Arad to be a mensch to herself *and* to others. *(Because Yael Arad showed respect for her body, she was able to bring happiness and pride to her country.)*

## Sh'mirat Habriyut Top 5

(pages 58–60)

### 1. Eat Mensch Food

Ask: Why do you think the Talmud forbids Jews to live in a city that does not contain a vegetable garden? (*Answers may include: because we should always have access to healthful food; because gardens provide food year after year; because gardens teach us to work together and share responsibility.*)

### 2. Get Movin'

Explain to your students that the yellow face in the middle has a "neutral" expression, to be used for activities that the student considers so-so. For fun, take a poll to determine the class's favorite activities.

### 3. Sleep Tight

Ask: Why do you think Jewish law considers depriving a neighbor of sleep stealing? (*Answers may include: Sleep is valuable; Jewish law considers our health very important.*)

### 4. Be a Danger Dodger

Explain that "don't rely on a miracle" means that each of us is responsible for thinking ahead. Invite students to share examples of times they chose not to participate in an activity for the sake of safety.

### 5. Balance Yourself

Have the class read the Hebrew blessing aloud. Explain that we are partners with God in sustaining our bodies; God may sustain us, but we must do what we can to keep ourselves safe.

## A Note of Middot: Self-Discipline

(page 61)

Tell your students that this *middah* is based on a lesson from *Pirkei Avot*, which teaches us to practice "moderation" and "a minimum of worldly pleasure." Ask: Why do you think the rabbis of *Pirkei Avot* taught us to moderate pleasures such as eating and sleeping? (*Though we must eat and sleep in order to live, too much of either can harm our health. We should enjoy each in moderation.*)

## As a Family

Copy and distribute the "Family Worksheet" found on the following page. During the next class session, have students share their family discussions with the class.

**Family Worksheet 3**

# Health Contract

Dear Parent:

In *A Kid's Mensch Handbook* we learned the mitzvah of *sh'mirat habriyut*, caring for our physical and emotional health. Ask your child to explain why Judaism considers caring for our bodies and minds an important obligation.

As a family, discuss how you each currently perform the mitzvah of *sh'mirat habriyut*—for example, by getting adequate rest, brushing your teeth regularly, and reaching out to others when you feel ill or stressed. Then consider ways in which you can support each other to expand your observance of the mitzvah. For example, how might you help one another develop better eating habits? What exercise can you participate in as a family?

You might want to write a contract in which each of you commits to observing an act of *sh'mirat habriyut* beyond what you currently do and pledge to support each other in fulfilling your commitments. For example, one person might commit to exercising three times a week, and the other members of the family could commit to helping that person make the time to do so.

If your family is comfortable with sharing its contract with our class, we would be pleased to have your child bring it in as a model for us.

Sincerely,

# Part Three

# Be a Mensch to Others

## Chapter 6

# Ready, Set, Mensch!

**Student text: pages 64–75**

## Overview

In Chapter 6, we learn how to treat others with respect through the mitzvah of *talmud Torah*—Jewish learning. *Talmud Torah* may be the most important mitzvah of all, because learning leads to action.

## Learning Objectives

Students will be able to:

- Describe how study has helped to unify and strengthen the Jewish community.
- Explain why Jewish tradition considers *talmud Torah* the most important mitzvah.
- Provide examples of how *talmud Torah* leads to action and describe ways to practice *talmud Torah* in their everyday lives.

## Vocabulary

**talmud Torah** the mitzvah of Jewish learning

**Torah lishma** learning for its own sake

## Set Induction

Draw an outline of a tree on the chalkboard. Tell your students: The Torah is often referred to as *Etz Ḥayim*, the Tree of Life, because it pro-vides nourishment and sustenance for the Jewish people. Ask: What are some ways the Torah provides nourishment for the Jewish people? *(Answers may include: Its laws teach us how to live our lives; it connects us to God; it provides us with wisdom and guidance.)* Write the responses on the chalkboard, inside the tree. Draw a fruit around each response, creating a fruit tree.

Explain that in this chapter we'll learn how the Torah has been a source of nourishment from generation to generation. The Torah and all of Jewish learning teaches us how to be *menschen* to others.

## First Things First (page 65)

Invite your students to talk about a time when they learned something new. Ask:

- Why is it important to begin with small steps and to practice? *(So we can become better and better.)*
- Why is this lesson important as we learn to become *menschen*? *(We must learn how to be* menschen *to others, then become better and better.)*

## The Tree of Knowledge (page 66)

Give your students as many as 10 minutes to complete this exercise, as some students may find it challenging to connect the skill in column 2 to the action in column 3. You might divide the class into pairs and sit with each pair for a minute or two, helping them to think of examples.

## Learning to the Rescue (page 67)

Teach your students a new word: *Diaspora*, which comes from the word "dispersion." Explain that for more than two thousand years, Jewish communities living outside Israel have comprised the Diaspora. Tell your students that even though we may live far from the Jewish homeland, all Jews look to the Torah as the source of law and wisdom.

### Photo Op

Point to the picture of the girl holding the Torah on page 67. Have a volunteer read the caption aloud. Ask: At what important moment in our lives do we read from the Torah for the first time? *(bar and bat mitzvah)* Explain that once we reach this important milestone, we become not only students but teachers, responsible for showing others how to become *menschen*.

### Expand the Conversation

Pick a volunteer to read aloud the "Quick Quote" at the bottom of page 67. Ask: What are some special Jewish times in the year when we take time to learn about our past? *(Answers may include: We remember our freedom from slavery during Passover; the miracle of the oil during Ḥanukkah; the birth of Israel during Yom Ha'atzma'ut.)*

## Mensch Spotlight (page 68)

Ask: What do *you* have in common with Rabbi Akiva? Have your students talk about times when they did the right thing though it may have been unpopular. What did they learn from the experience?

## The Most Important Mitzvah (page 69)

Ask a student to read aloud the Hebrew inside the "Mensch-ifying Glass". To eliminate confusion, explain that the Talmud is an important set of books that contain Jewish law; the Hebrew word *talmud* means "learning." *Talmud Torah* refers to Jewish learning in general, not the set of books.

### Bring It to Life

Divide the class into groups of 2 or 3. On the board, write: Hebrew, Jewish history, and Israel. Instruct students to list as many Jewish subjects as they can in 2 minutes. Then have a representative from each group share their group's list with the class. Write the subjects on the board. If students don't name them, be sure to include: Jewish holidays, Jewish values, and of course, Torah.

Explain that even learning about our families and our heritage may be considered *talmud Torah*.

## Photo Op

Point to the picture of the students on page 69. Have a volunteer read the caption aloud. Ask each student to name one goal he or she has for the future. Ask: What must you learn in order to achieve that goal?

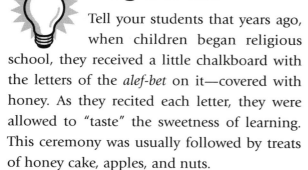

## Bring It to Life

Tell your students that years ago, when children began religious school, they received a little chalkboard with the letters of the *alef-bet* on it—covered with honey. As they recited each letter, they were allowed to "taste" the sweetness of learning. This ceremony was usually followed by treats of honey cake, apples, and nuts.

Use this story as a springboard to hold a celebration of the chapter's lesson in your classroom. You and your class can bring in sweet treats to emphasize the sweetness of *talmud Torah*.

## Mount Mitzvah (page 71)

Point out that students should begin the exercise from the bottom, then "climb" the mountain by connecting the three levels.

### Answers

- *Sh'mirat habriyut* ➡ Eat well ➡ happy and healthy bodies
- *Derech eretz* ➡ Welcome guests ➡ guests feel welcome
- *Dibbuk ḥaverim* ➡ Respect classmates ➡ good friends

## Talmud Torah Top 5 (pages 72–74)

### 1. Follow the Leader

Once they've completed their lists, each student should choose the description he or she considers the most important. Ask students to explain their answers.

### 2. Study with a Buddy

Ask students to explain how friends and study companions can also be teachers. Tell your class that later in the book we'll spend a whole chapter describing how to be a good friend.

### 3. Set Aside Time

Your students may add additional hours—either before 3 p.m. or after 8 p.m. Have them add the hours in the green space around the time chart. Congratulate them on the learning they are doing, and encourage them to do more.

### 4. Learn for Fun

Ask: How does improving your skills also help to improve your self-respect? How can it help you to be a role model to others?

### 5. Pass It On

Have each student present a 2 to 3 minute lesson on the subject of his or her choice. (Suggest: how to play an instrument, a sport, or a video game.) After each presentation, ask the rest of the class: What did you learn? Ask the student: What did you learn from teaching? After all the presentations, point out how much the class learned in a short period of time. Who knows? Perhaps the exercise will inspire future teachers.

# A Note of Middot: Humility

**(page 75)**

Remind your students of a symbol of humility we perform during worship services. Near the end of the service, when we recite the Aleinu, we bow as we say:

*Va'anachnu korim, umishtaḥavim umodim lifnei melech malchei hamlachim.*

We bend the knee, bow, and give thanks before the Ruler of rulers.

Ask: Why do you think we bow? *(To show our humility before God.)*

## As a Family

Invite your students' families to come to class with their children. Bring the families to the synagogue library. Share the story about the sweetness of learning on page 32 of this Teaching Guide. Encourage them to borrow a book, video, or musical recording, and to browse through the Jewish newspapers and magazines. Make the occasion festive: Serve food and perhaps invite your cantor or music director to teach some Israeli music.

# Be a Mensch to Your Family

## Overview

In Chapter 7, we learn to treat our families respectfully with the value of *sh'lom bayit*—peace in the home. Through *sh'lom bayit*, we practice the qualities of forgiveness, responsibility, and patience.

## Learning Objectives

Your students will be able to:

- Define *sh'lom bayit* and explain its importance.
- Discuss why respect for parents and siblings is essential to a peaceful home.
- List practical ways to be a responsible and respectful family member.

## Vocabulary

**erech apayim** "slowness to anger"; the value of patience

**kibbud av v'em** "Honor your father and mother"; the Fifth Commandment

**sh'lom bayit** "peace in the home"

## Set Induction

Ask your students to complete the following sentence silently, in their heads or on a sheet of paper: My favorite family memories are….

Allow students to share their memories with the class. Ask: What made the events or moments special? How were members of your family *menschen* to one another at the time?

Explain that in this chapter, we'll learn about *sh'lom bayit*, the mitzvah that can help us to create positive, happy memories every day.

## The Family Mensch (page 77)

*Note:* Have students read the phrases in purple as a continuous sentence, ending with "be tolerant."

After your students have finished reading this page aloud, point out that Joseph *chose* to tell his dream to his family. Ask:

- How did Joseph's choice affect his family?
- What could his brothers have done to preserve family peace?
- What could Jacob, Joseph's father, have done to help prevent the conflict?

Encourage your students to use the words *kindness* and *respect* in their answers.

## Home Sweet Home (page 78)

Allow your students 5 to 10 minutes to complete this exercise, as it contains questions that require reflection.

> **Note:** Be aware that students may be experiencing difficult family situations, including divorce and death. Be sensitive to your students' reactions and emotions. If a student prefers not to share, please respect his or her privacy.

### Bring It to Life

Have each student create a "family paper chain." Provide the class with light-colored construction paper, scissors, markers, and staplers. Ask students to cut the construction paper into strips.

Instruct each student to write his or her own name on one strip of paper, then write the names of close family members on other strips (using one strip for each person). Students will write adjectives that describe each person on each strip. Instruct students to staple their strips into chains, then share the chains with the class.

## The Magic Word (page 79)

Before reading this section, have a student read the Hebrew inside the "Mensch-ifying Glass" aloud. Your students will likely know that *shalom* means "peace." Tell them that *bayit* means "house" or "home." Ask: What are some ways to create a peaceful home? *(Answers may include: helping around the house; sharing with siblings; doing nice things for our parents.)*

## Mensch Cake Recipe (page 80)

Invite students to share their mensch cake recipes with the class.

Tell your students that home is the ideal place to practice The Golden Rule: *v'ahavta l'reacha kamocha*—love your neighbor as yourself.

## Mom and Dad: Partners in Creation (page 81)

Write the Ten Commandments on the board, or post them in the classroom:

### Tablet 1:

1. I am Adonai your God who brought you out of Egypt.
2. Do not have any other gods besides Me or pray to idols.
3. Do not use My name except for holy purposes.
4. Remember Shabbat and keep it holy.
5. Honor your father and mother.

### Tablet 2:

6. Do not murder.
7. Do not commit adultery.
8. Do not steal.
9. Do not swear falsely.
10. Do not desire what belongs to your neighbor.

Point out the observation made by Rabbi Loew: The Commandments on tablet 1 have to do with our relationship with God; the Commandments on tablet 2 have to do with our relationships with one another. Only the Fifth Commandment, "Honor your father and mother," seems out of place. Remind your students that when we honor our parents, we also honor God.

## Expand the Conversation

Read the following quote from Rabbi Shimon bar Yoḥai to your class: "The most difficult of all *mitzvot* is 'Honor your father and mother.'" Ask: What do you think he meant by this? (*Answers may include: because we must honor our parents every day; we should respect them even if we disagree with them.*)

## Photo Op

Point to the photo on page 81. Have a student read the caption aloud. Ask: What are some gifts a parent can give to a child? Encourage your students to describe gifts that are not material, such as a sense of honesty, fair play, respect for others, or a connection to their Jewish heritage.

## Brothers and Sisters: Friends for Life (page 82–83)

Say: Raise your hand if you've ever had a disagreement with a brother or sister. (All or most hands will go up.) Ask: How would a mensch handle a disagreement or an argument with a

sibling? (*A mensch would listen, be patient, and protect* sh'lom bayit.)

## Bring It to Life

Have students think of ways to strengthen *sh'lom bayit* with their siblings. Write their ideas on the board. Begin by writing: knock before entering a sibling's room; be patient when a sibling needs our help.

## Sh'lom Bayit Top 5 (pages 84–86)

### 1. Always Speak Respectfully to Mom and Dad

Have students act out the following scenarios. In each case, one should play the child, another the parent.

- A friend invites you to the movies. Your parent wants you to stay home because your aunt is visiting from Australia. Discuss the issue calmly, and offer a reasonable compromise that respects your parent and your visitor.

- You want to adopt a puppy. Your parent is concerned that you will lose interest in it. Provide your parent with a plan to take care of it. Make sure to address your parent's concerns.

- Your parent won't let you wear your favorite T-shirt to Shabbat dinner. Always show respect for your parent's decision.

### 2. Be a Team Player

Invite volunteers to share their responses with the class. Make a list of "family no-no's" on the board, including yelling, name-calling, and ignoring others.

### 3. Do Fun Family Stuff

You may wish to distribute markers and sheets of paper to allow students more room to record their favorite family memories.

### 4. Forgive and Forget

Ask: Which do you think is harder—forgiving or apologizing? Tell your students that both involve courage and compromise—and both strengthen *sh'lom bayit*.

### 5. Be a Family Rep

Say: Imagine that a family friend calls you a mensch in front of your parents. How do you think your parents feel? How do you feel? Tell your students that a great way to strengthen *sh'lom bayit* is by being a mensch at home and away from home!

## A Note of Middot: Patience
**(page 87)**

Have your students share examples of pet peeves, such as siblings who enter their rooms without asking, or having to wash the dishes. Have their classmates suggest positive ways to apply patience to the situation, such as speaking calmly and listening to the other person.

## As a Family

Copy and distribute the "Family Worksheet" on the following page. Have students complete the "*Sh'lom Bayit* Contract" with their families. During the next class session, have students share some of their family agreements with the class.

**Family Worksheet 4**

# Sh'lom Bayit Contract

Dear Parent:

In *A Kid's Mensch Handbook* we learned about the mitzvah of *sh'lom bayit*—peace in the home. We learned that a mensch is respectful, cooperative, and patient with family members.

As a family, complete the following *"Sh'lom Bayit* Contract." Have each family member contribute at least one way to strengthen *sh'lom bayit* in *your* home. Examples include: be honest with one another; speak to one another respectfully; respect one another's privacy.

Sign the contract, then hang it in the kitchen or another room where the whole family can see it every day.

## Sh'lom Bayit (Peace in the Home) Contract

**for the** _____ **Family**

We pledge to strengthen and preserve *sh'lom bayit* in the following ways:

1. _____

2. _____

3. _____

4. _____

5. _____

Signed: _____        _____

_____        _____

# Be a Mensch to Your Friends and Classmates

**Student Text: pages 88–99**

## Overview

In Chapter 8, we learn to treat friends and classmates respectfully with the value of *dibbuk haverim*—attachment to friends. Through *dibbuk haverim*, we help one another to be our best selves and to reach our greatest potential.

## Learning Objectives

Students will be able to:

- Explain the importance of respect, trust, and honesty in our interactions with friends and classmates.

- Define and discuss the value of *dibbuk haverim*.

- Give examples of how they can practice *dibbuk haverim* in their own lives.

## Vocabulary

**dibbuk haverim** "attachment to friends"; the value of friendship

**hevruta** study pairs or groups; from the word *haver*, "friend"

**kavanah** "concentration" or "focus"

**p'sharah** "compromise"; from the same root as *pashor*, "melt"

## Set Induction

Explain that in this chapter, we'll learn the value of respect and kindness among friends and classmates.

To introduce the lesson, copy and distribute "Buddy Bingo" on page 43 of this Teaching Guide. Explain the game in this way:

- "Buddy Bingo" is just like regular bingo, except the cards do not contain preprinted numbers. Instead, there are descriptions that apply to your classmates or to their families.

- Your challenge is to find students that fit the descriptions in the "Buddy Bingo" squares.

- Each time you find a student who conforms to the description in the box, have him or her sign inside the box. Each classmate's name may be used twice. You may use your own name once.

- You have 15 minutes to fill as many boxes as you can.

After 15 minutes, call out individual students' names, one at a time. Students should mark off the corresponding square, one square at a time. (You may need to call each student's name more than once.) Continue calling out names until someone has marked off any five spaces in a row—across, down, or diagonally.

If time allows, play for second and third places. You may wish to have a small prize ready for the winners, as well as for the rest of the class!

## Superfriend (page 89)

Ask: How is Rachel a mensch through taking action? (*She makes students feel welcome and accepted; she sticks up for people who are being picked on; she starts school clubs.*)

Point out that Rachel's values did not change from person to person; she was a good friend to everyone.

## Expand the Conversation

Pick a volunteer to read aloud the "Quick Quote" on page 89. Ask: Why is it "heroic" to turn an enemy into a friend? (*Because it requires more effort—and courage—to make a friend of a rival or a former friend.*)

## Mensch-o-meter (page 90)

Allow students to spend 5 to 10 minutes on the first part of this exercise. Tell them to compare their Mensch-o-meters with their classmates, and to reflect on their choices.

Have students work individually on the second part of the exercise to think of qualities they would like to embody.

## Friend for Sale (page 91)

Ask: What are some examples of nonmaterial gifts that we can give to friends? (*Answers may include: companionship, comfort, guidance, or praise.*)

After reading each bulleted item, invite students to share examples of ways they made or strengthened a friendship through loyalty, honesty, or attention.

## Photo Op

Have a volunteer read the photo caption on page 91 aloud. Tell students to complete Joseph Zabara's quote in their own way: "Friendship is like _____." You may have students write their answers, then use the sentence as the first line of a poem.

## A Treasure (page 92)

Ask a student to read the Hebrew inside the "Mensch-ifying Glass" aloud. Ask: How does *dibbuk ḥaverim* help us to perform *mitzvot*? Have your students describe times when they went the extra mile to do something nice for a friend.

## Bring It to Life

Create a "*Dibbuk Ḥaverim* Declaration." Using markers and a sheet of poster paper, your students will write: "We, the members of [name of teacher or class] hereby pledge to _____." Have students create a list of ways to be a good friend or classmate. Then have the entire class sign the declaration. Hang the *"Dibbuk Ḥaverim Declaration"* in a visible place in your classroom.

If time allows, tell your students to read and explain the *"Dibbuk Ḥaverim* Declaration" to a younger class.

## Win-Win (pages 93–94)

Ask students to think about a time when a friend corrected them. How did they feel? Give students a few minutes to record this memory in "A Friend Indeed" (page 94).

## Dibbuk Ḥaverim Top 5 (pages 95–98)

### 1. Be Friendly

Request that students use the phrase *dibbuk ḥaverim* in their written responses. Invite volunteers to share their responses with the class.

### 2. Meet in the Middle

After they've completed the exercise, ask students to think of times when a mensch should *not* compromise—for example, when a friend wants to play video games instead of doing homework.

### 3. Keep a Secret Safe

Tell your students: Become more sensitive to *l'shon hara*—gossip. Recognize that you are listening to it, or that you are speaking it yourself. Before making a statement about someone, ask yourself these three questions:

a. Is it true?
b. Is it well-meaning?
c. Is it unlikely to hurt or insult someone?

If a statement doesn't receive a "yes" to all three questions—best not to say it.

### 4. Listen Up!

Have students act out two scenarios: one in which one person speaks and the other listens with *kavanah*—concentration—and one in which one person speaks and the other looks around, whistles, or looks at his or her watch. Ask the class: Why is it important for a mensch to be a good listener?

### 5. Be Grateful for Your Friends

Recite the Sheheḥeyanu as a class. Tell your students that *lazman hazeh* means "to this time." The blessing helps us to make special moments holy.

## A Note of Middot: Cooperation (page 99)

Have your students work together to create a new holiday: *Yom Middot* (Jewish Values Day). Tell your students that they must:

• Choose a date for the new holiday.

• Describe games or activities for the holiday.

• Choose a theme song for the holiday (either an existing song, or an original composition).

• Explain the importance of the holiday.

If time allows, give your students 30 minutes to complete the exercise. Rather than assigning specific tasks, instruct students to complete the exercise through teamwork.

After they've completed the exercise, tell the class to present the new holiday to you. Then ask:

- What did the exercise teach you about cooperation?

- What must people do in order to cooperate?

- What must they *not* do?

 ## As a Family

Have your students talk to their families about one of the most dangerous challenges to friendship: *l'shon hara*—gossip.

Your students should explain to their families that *l'shon hara* is a damaging statement that is said for a mean or hurtful purpose. Have them discuss this idea over dinner and think of ways to work as a family to make their home a *l'shon hara*-free environment.

During the next class session, invite your students to report their conversations to the class.

# Buddy Bingo

| | | | | |
|---|---|---|---|---|
| I love chocolate ice cream.<br><br>Sign: _____ | I can find Israel on a map.<br><br>Sign: _____ | I can name everyone in the class.<br><br>Sign: _____ | Last Ḥanukkah, I lit the candles on the menorah.<br><br>Sign: _____ | I play a musical instrument.<br><br>Sign: _____ |
| I shook the *lulav* and *etrog* last Sukkot.<br><br>Sign: _____ | I know what *sh'lom bayit* means.<br><br>Sign: _____ | My favorite color is blue.<br><br>Sign: _____ | I go to a Jewish summer camp.<br><br>Sign: _____ | I listen to the radio in the morning.<br><br>Sign: _____ |
| I have two brothers.<br><br>Sign: _____ | I like latkes more than french fries.<br><br>Sign: _____ | **FREE** | I know my Hebrew name.<br><br>Sign: _____ | I have two sisters.<br><br>Sign: _____ |
| I have a dog and a cat.<br><br>Sign: _____ | I know what The Golden Rule is.<br><br>Sign: _____ | I've traveled to a foreign country.<br><br>Sign: _____ | I can name the last three U.S. presidents.<br><br>Sign: _____ | I know what *sh'mirat habriyut* means.<br><br>Sign: _____ |
| I know what *talmud Torah* means.<br><br>Sign: _____ | I play a sport at school.<br><br>Sign: _____ | I can name two Jewish movie stars.<br><br>Sign: _____ | I like summer more than winter.<br><br>Sign: _____ | I became friends with a new person at school this year.<br><br>Sign: _____ |

# Be a Mensch to Everyone

**Student Text: pages 100–111**

## Overview

In Chapter 9, we acquire four essential tools every mensch should have: *k'vod habriyot*—respect for all people; *derech eretz*—good manners; *klal Yisrael*—support for the world Jewish community; and *tzedakah*—righteous giving.

## Learning Objectives

Students will be able to:

- Explain how every mitzvah helps to repair the world.

- Define and provide examples of four new Jewish values: *k'vod habriyot*, *derech eretz*, *klal Yisrael*, and tzedakah.

- Understand the importance of being a mensch for its own sake.

## Vocabulary

**derech eretz** good manners; everyday courtesy

**klal Yisrael** the world Jewish community

**k'vod habriyot** "respect for all people"

**tikkun olam** "repairing the world"; the concept that each person is responsible for making the world a better place

## Set Induction

Read aloud this quote from the chapter: "I always give much away, and so gather happiness instead of pleasure."

Illustrate the difference between happiness and pleasure in this way:

- Have your students describe the *pleasure* they experience when eating their favorite dinner.

- They should then describe the *happiness* they experience when delivering dinner to a needy family.

Ask your students to provide additional examples of the difference between happiness and pleasure. Explain that this chapter will be about the happiness we feel and create through being a mensch.

## One Piece at a Time (page 101)

Ask: According to Rabbi Luria's version of the world's creation, why are *mitzvot* important? (*Every mitzvah helps to repair the world.*)

## Repairing the World (page 102)

Help your students complete the last section of this exercise with these examples of repair jobs:

- Choosing a career that helps others, such as medicine or education. Explain that we can bring generosity and kindness to many professions.

- Having a positive effect on others by being cheerful or helping people through their problems.

- Being helpful at home and in the community.

## K'vod Habriyot: Respect for All People (page 103)

Ask these rhetorical questions: How many candles can one flame light? How many people can you show respect for, once you have *k'vod habriyot*?

Have a student read the Hebrew inside the "Mensch-ifying Glass" aloud. Explain that in its broadest sense, *habriyot* can mean "all creation"; we use it here to mean "all people."

## The Kavod Railroad (page 104)

Your students may be interested to know that a mitzvah exists for animals: *tza'ar ba'alei ḥayim*, which teaches us to prevent the suffering of all living beings.

### Bring It to Life

To illustrate the "contagious" quality of *kavod*, bring dominoes to class. Stand one domino on a large table or on the floor and say: "I place a dollar in the tzedakah box."

Invite students to continue the story by placing additional steps, one next to the other. (Examples include: The dollar goes toward curing a disease; one child who was ill is now cured; she grows up to be a doctor; etc.) Students should add one domino for each new step. Once the class has exhausted its ideas (or dominoes), tip the first domino and watch the "Kavod Railroad" go!

## Derech Eretz: The Mensch Way (page 105)

Explain that the literal translation of *derech eretz* is "the way of the land"; *derech eretz* teaches us the *way* or *manner* in which we should treat others in everyday interactions.

## Mensch Manners (page 106)

Invite students to share their *derech eretz* ideas with the class.

Divide the class into groups of 2 or 3. Have each group list as many ways as they can to practice *derech eretz*. See who can list the most ways in 5 minutes.

## Klal Yisrael: One Big Family (pages 107–108)

Ask: In what ways is *klal Yisrael*—the world Jewish community—like one big family? *(Answers may include: We share the same homeland—Israel; we respect one another; we are responsible for one another; it is important to stick together, even though we may disagree.)*

### Bring It to Life

Here are some ideas to bring Israel to life in your classroom:

1. *Create a Hebrew-rich environment.* Infuse classroom discussions with as many Hebrew words and phrases as you can. When students enter the room, say *shalom*; when they leave, say *l'hitra'ot*—see you later!

2. *Bring in Israeli food and music.* Bring in pita and hummus; play CDs of Israeli music;

invite an Israeli dance teacher to your class to teach a few steps.

3. *Invite an Israeli to speak to your class.* Welcome an Israeli (teens are best!) to speak to your class about life in Israel. Help your students to see that their lives are similar to those of Israeli kids: They like to play video games, talk on the phone, watch TV, and use e-mail, too!

### Photo Op

Point to the photograph of the Israeli scouts on page 108. Ask: What words would you use to describe the expressions on the faces of the Israeli scouts? *(Answers may include: proud, happy, welcoming.)*

Remind students that Jews all over the world consider Israel their second home.

### Mensch Spotlight (page 109)

Ask: In what way did *klal Yisrael* and *k'vod habriyot* influence Henrietta Szold's actions? *(She worked not only to help Jews but Arabs of Palestine as well.)*

### Expand the Conversation

Tell your students that in addition to Henrietta Szold's important work for Israel, during the 1930s she created an organization called Youth Aliyah, which saved more than 20,000 children from the Holocaust.

### Tzedakah: The Right Thing (page 110)

Review the first paragraph by asking: What is the difference between charity and tzedakah? *(We give charity because we want to; we give tzedakah because we are obliged to give to those in need.)*

### Tzedakah Supreme (page 111)

Have students read the list, starting with #1. Have them provide specific examples for each.

### Expand the Conversation

Tell your students that Jewish tradition not only requires us to give to the less fortunate; it also demands that we respect their dignity, that is, save them from embarrassment. In biblical times, farmers followed the Torah's instruction to leave the harvest of the corners of the field for the poor so that they would not have to beg.

# Special Sections

## Mensch Magic (pages 112–113)

Involve the entire class in reading this section. Have students sit in a circle and alternate reading sentences aloud, then have the class read the bulleted list in unison.

The following questions will help your students reflect on the book's lessons.

- For you, what was the most memorable lesson in *A Kid's Mensch Handbook*?
- What new ways to be a mensch did you learn in *A Kid's Mensch Handbook*?
- How do you plan to make your own "mensch-ful splash"?

## Mensch Diploma (pages 114–115)

Have your students complete their Mensch Diplomas. Then collect the books and fill in the date and name lines.

Congratulate your students on completing the book and on acquiring valuable knowledge from our Jewish ancestors, one another, and themselves.

Mazal Tov!

## As a Family

Plan a ceremony to which you may invite parents, your principal, rabbi, cantor, or any other special guests.

Then, one at a time, call each of your students up to the front of the class to receive his or her book with the completed certificate. You may wish to compose a short speech for each student—for example, "To Rebecca, for her unique contribution to our discussion of the 'all-in-one' mitzvah." Or, you may want to ask each student to share something he or she learned about being a mensch. If you do, prepare your students by asking them to write out one or two sentences in advance.

When all your students are standing at the front of the room, you and your guests may recite the Sheheḥeyanu blessing, which appears on page 98 of *A Kid's Mensch Handbook*.

# Notes